Exploring the Past

Childcraft

1989 Edition
Childcraft

Copyright © 1987 by World Book, Inc.
World Book House
77 Mount Ephraim
Tunbridge Wells
Kent TN4 8AZ, UK.

Portions of the text and certain illustrations previously
published under the title of **Childcraft** – The How and
Why Library.
Copyright © 1985, USA by World Book, Inc.
Merchandise Mart Plaza, Chicago, Illinois 60654, USA.
International Copyright © 1985 by World Book, Inc.

Printed in the USA.

ISBN 0-7166-6003-2

World Book (Australia) Pty. Ltd.
World Book House
71–73 Lithgow Street
St. Leonards
New South Wales 2065.

Volume 13

Exploring
the Past

World Book, Inc.
a Scott Fetzer company
Chicago London Sydney
Toronto

Contents

When history began

How did the world begin? Where did we come from? People have been puzzling over questions like these for thousands of years.

The Bible tells of the Creation of the world in the Book of Genesis. It tells how God created the world and all living things.

But there are other stories about how the world began that have been told by people from many lands and with many different beliefs. These stories, which are very old, tell us a great deal about the people who first told them and the places where these people lived.

There is also a new story that scientists from different lands are still trying to put together. Some people do not agree with this scientific story. But most scientists think it is true.

Scientists tell us the earliest man-like creatures were alive about 14 million years ago. They were more like apes than people, but they did move about on two feet looking for food.

Some types of early people, like Nutcracker Man, did not survive. Those that did had changed their way of life. They moved out of Africa, into Asia and Europe. They became meat eaters and they learnt to hunt in groups and to share their food. They used sharp flint and stone tools.

About 40,000 years ago modern people appeared. Their brain was the same size as ours today and they behaved more like us. They were able to make finer tools to help them to hunt, they buried their dead, and painted the walls of the caves where they lived.

Later, about 10,000 years ago, people began to farm. They stayed in one place and began to live in groups called communities.

People have certainly made an impact on this earth. We've been around for a long time, but in the history of the earth we're really late arrivals.

Imagine all of earth's history squeezed into one day. On this scale the tiniest living things probably first appeared at about 4 am. But the first animals with backbones — fishes — don't appear until about 9.20 pm. Man-like apes appear one minute before midnight — and modern people less than one second before midnight strikes!

Nutcracker Man

There was a rustling in the tall grass. Then a face poked out. It was a hairy face with huge jaws and tiny, round eyes.

Carefully the creature moved forwards on his back legs, looking for something to eat.

He was used to searching for food like this. He could run on two feet instead of four. What's more, he had two arms free which he used to carry things. When he found food, he could carry it back to the trees. In the shelter of the trees and bushes he was safe from attacks by other animals.

What was this creature? Was he an ape or was he a man? Really he was neither. Perhaps it is best to call him an ape-man. He lived many thousands of years ago in Africa – long before there were any true people living there. Because of his big jaws and teeth, scientists have named him Nutcracker Man.

Into the unknown

The people huddled in the little boat were very frightened. They had never been so far from the land before. On every side of them there was nothing but water. But they were brave people and they had set out to see what was over the horizon. Was there land there, or did the sea go on for ever? The strong wind and currents moved the boat along, further and further away from home.

Suddenly there was a shout, and one of the men pointed ahead. Straining their eyes, they saw a dark line in the distance. Here was land at last!

Over the centuries, people spread overland
from Africa into the great empty spaces of
Europe and Asia. Then, one million years ago,
the earth entered an Ice Age. Huge sheets of ice
spread out from the North and South Poles and
from the high mountains. In time, the ice
covered much of the northern and southern
parts of the world. The people who lived at
this time must have found life very hard.
As their numbers grew, they moved to fresh
land in search of food and fuel. When the ice
retreated, they followed it northwards. When
they could travel no further on foot, they
learned to build boats and brave the open sea
for the very first time. In this way they
discovered land where no human had ever
been before.

The mammoth hunters

The man crept silently through the trees. All the time he was looking about him. Suddenly he stood still, watching and waiting. Then he lifted his arm and flung the spear as hard as he could. He hit his target – and the animal went down.

Hunting was difficult and dangerous for prehistoric people. The only weapons they had were spears or bows and arrows with sharp tips made of flint. The hunters had to move very quietly to catch alert, fast-running animals like deer and boar. They had to get close enough to throw their spears and make sure of a meal.

They also hunted the mammoth, a kind of elephant about four metres high with long tusks. Its thick skin and shaggy coat were too tough for spears and arrows to pierce, so the

A **hand-axe** is made by chipping flakes off a large flint stone. The axe has a sharp point and edges. It is used by holding it cupped in the hand. Some of the flakes are also used as **knives** or **scrapers**.

hunters had another way of catching this animal. They used fire. They set light to bushes and tall grass, driving the terrified mammoth into swamps and rivers. Here the mammoth got stuck and was left to die. Later it was cut up for food.

These big animals provided meat for many people. Their skins were also used to make clothes or tent coverings. The needles used to stitch the skins together were made from sharp splinters of bone.

A group of hunters didn't stay in one place for very long. In a short time they would have killed most of the animals and burnt up all the fuel in that area. Then they packed up their tools and skin tents and moved on to the next place in search of food.

Drawings on the wall

It was cold and damp in the cave. A trickle of water oozed down the wall, but the man didn't notice. He put down his simple lamp and looked at the ceiling. Above him was a row of bulky, horned bulls, and next to them were boars, stags and horses racing across the stone. The cave was alive with marvellous paintings of all the animals a prehistoric hunter could dream of.

Next the man began to make some paint. On a flat stone, he carefully mixed some powdered charcoal and then some red and brown rock dust with animal fat. Then, using his fingers and some feathers as a paint-brush, he made the shape of a huge bison on the cave wall. And in the flickering light of the lamp, it almost seemed the great animal was moving.

Prehistoric paintings like these have been found in caves in many parts of France, Spain, North Africa and Australia. Some of them are as much as 30,000 years old. They have been preserved in the caves, where there is no wind, rain or sunlight to wear them away, for all those thousands of years.

Most of the paintings are of prehistoric animals like woolly mammoths and rhinoceroses, and of bison, horses and deer. Very few show people. No one knows exactly why the pictures were made. Some scientists think the prehistoric people used the paintings to make magic – magic they believed could help them when they went hunting. Others think the animals were meant to stand for something else, like spirits or gods.

The first farmers

One day about 9,000 BC – that's about 11,000 years ago – a little boy was out walking. He picked some grains of wheat which were growing wild. As usual, when he got back to the camp where he lived, he gave the grains to his mother. She ground them into flour between two flat stones. But no one noticed that a few of the grains fell on to the earth.

Weeks later, when the family was wandering in search of food, they passed by their old camp. There, as if by magic, was a little clump of green shoots. More wheat! The fallen grains had sprouted and begun to grow. Soon there would be new grains of wheat to pick. The family had made a great discovery – instead of having to search for wild food, they could grow it themselves in one place.

And so they settled down. They gathered more wild grains and planted them in the ground. They built huts with sticks covered in mud. They even built storehouses to keep their spare food in. As time went by, they learned

how to keep goats and sheep in herds nearby.
Now they could have meat and milk whenever
they liked.

This was probably the way farming began.
It was one of the most important changes in
human history. People no longer needed to
wander about in search of food. They could
stay in one place and farm the land. And with
food to spare, they had
time to invent new
skills such as pottery
and weaving.

The early civilizations

A great **Sumerian** temple, called a ziggurat.

Think about all the things you've been doing lately. Have you been reading? Writing? Studying? Praying? Playing? You are sure to have done some of these things. Most people's lives today are filled with such activities. They are the activities of a civilization. But it hasn't always been like this.

At first, people were only hunters or farmers. Then, as time passed, farming began to solve the food problem. People grew more food than was needed each day. So they could store some away. Now there was time for new activities and skills to be learnt.

The next big step was for people to get together and work out laws to live by and ways of sharing and recording their knowledge. This was the beginning of civilization.

The first civilization grew up about 6,000 years ago in Sumer. Today this area is called Iraq. Other early civilizations followed in India, Egypt and China.

The Hanging Gardens of **Babylon**.

The Great Bath at Mohenjodaro in the **Indus Valley**.

The Sumerians developed farming machines and skills. Cities developed and here the earliest forms of metal work, brick building, writing and money began.

In India the Indus Valley civilization developed along the banks of the rivers in western India and Pakistan. Later civilizations also spread along the River Ganges.

The tombs of **Ancient Egypt**.

The Egyptians believed in everlasting life. The Egyptian kings, called pharaohs, built tombs inside enormous stone pyramids. The records of their lives are still being unearthed today from these burial places.

The great area of the Far East had been divided by wars. Now the Ch'in tribe succeeded in uniting everyone into one vast empire called China.

The tomb of the royal Ming family of **China**.

All these places had something in common — they all had great rivers, which made the land good for farming. The easier it was for people to farm land and get food, the more time they had left for other things.

In the next part of the book, we will look at these early civilizations and read about some of their new activities and exciting skills.

Hanging gardens

About 2,500 years ago, King Nebuchadnezzar ruled the land called Babylonia. He married a beautiful princess from another country and brought her to Babylon, the capital of Babylonia. But the new queen grew homesick for the mountains and gardens of her homeland. So the king called together his architects and craftsmen because he had a plan. "Build me the most wonderful gardens in the world," he told them.

The work began. The king's men built tall walls with terraces on top, where they planted flowers and fruit trees. They made beautiful fountains which sparkled against the green leaves. The gardens were as high as a building with thirty-five storeys.

It was a hard task without machinery. The men had to haul huge stones and rocks from far away to build the walls and terraces. And they had to pump water from the river to keep the gardens green and the fountains flowing.

We don't know how much of this story is true. But we do know from ancient writings that the Hanging Gardens of Babylon did exist.

Along with six other man-made marvels, the **Hanging Gardens of Babylon** are remembered as one of the Seven Wonders of the Ancient World.

Building the pyramids

At Giza, near the River Nile in Egypt, stand three huge pyramids. They are all that's left of the Seven Wonders of the Ancient World. The other wonders were destroyed long ago. But the pyramids are so massive that it's hard to see how they could ever fall down.

Why were they built? They were made as huge tombs for the kings of Egypt. The Egyptians believed in life after death, so when the kings were buried their bodies were specially preserved. Food and drink were buried with them to make sure that the kings survived their journey to the next world.

Imagine how difficult it must have been to put up such buildings so long ago! There were no cranes, no bulldozers and no iron tools in those days. The only tools were simple ones — copper chisels and saws, stone hammers and wooden set-squares. But what the Egyptians did have was plenty of muscle-power, and hundreds of thousands of men were used as labourers. They cut vast blocks of stone from nearby quarries and hauled the blocks on rollers or sledges over land.

Other huge blocks were brought by water on enormous barges. As the pyramid grew higher, great slopes of sand were heaped up at the sides. The stones were pulled up these sand ramps into position. When the building was finished, the ramps were dug away again, leaving the giant monument standing alone.

Watcher on the Nile

As the sun rose higher in the sky, the priest
hurried down to the river.

Today was the day! It was the beginning of
spring and soon the great River Nile would
begin to rise. Then it would burst its banks and
flood the fields. Every year the Egyptians
waited eagerly for this moment. They knew
that the floods would water the fields and
leave a layer of rich mud on top. Later, crops
could be planted in this good soil to provide
food for the people.

Sometimes though, the Nile didn't rise high
enough. The fields dried up and the crops
were poor. Other times the river rose too far.
The raging waters swept through the villages,
tearing down houses and spoiling the stores of
food.

At last the priest reached the edge of the river and he bent down to stare at some marks carved into the bank. The marks were part of a measuring instrument called a nilometer. As the water rose, it slowly covered up the marks one by one.

Had the water risen today? Yes! It was up to the next mark. The floods had begun. The priest knew he must spread the news because the villagers would want to show their thanks to the river god, Osiris. They would all bring presents to throw into the water. After all, if the people did not give thanks, the god might be angry and stop the floods. So the priest ran back to tell the villagers his news.

The secret village

It was early morning and the sun was already high in the sky. As the workers trudged along the path, they knew it was going to be another hot, tiring day.

The men lived in a village in Egypt. It was a secret village, hidden in a desert valley. Every morning they were taken out to work, and every evening they came back to the village. At night, guards stood at the gates to make sure that no one came in or out.

The villagers were building a tomb in the desert. Some were miners who dug long, winding tunnels into the hillside. Others were artists who painted the tunnel walls with strange and beautiful pictures. And others were craftsmen who made statues and wonderful ornaments.

Why did they live in secret? Well, the tomb was being made for the king of Egypt. All Egyptian kings were buried in very grand tombs, filled with many treasures. Some were even inside great stone pyramids. The kings planned their tombs themselves, and had them built while they were still alive. After they were buried the tombs were sealed up. But robbers always broke in and stole the treasure.

Then one king called Thutmose, thought of a new plan. He would build his tomb in a valley, far away from the towns. After he was buried the entrance would be covered with sand and rocks. Nobody would know it was there – nobody, of course, except the men who built it. And they had to promise to keep the place a secret.

But the secret didn't last for ever as King Thutmose had hoped. In the end robbers did break into the tomb. They stole what they could and smashed the rest. Now those great treasures have disappeared, but the tomb is still there with its own story to tell.

Under the bodhi tree

Young Prince Gautama lived in India long ago. He was handsome and clever and very rich. He had a beautiful wife. The prince enjoyed himself, eating and drinking and lazing about the palace.

One day in the street he saw a figure hobbling along. It was an old man, bent and leaning on a stick. Further on, the prince met a young man, pale and sick with disease. Nearby was something lying on the ground – a dead body.

Gautama was horrified. In all his happy life he had never before seen anyone unhappy or in pain. Now he saw that most people had lives full of sadness and suffering. Why was this so? He decided that he would find out. That night he slipped secretly out of his palace. He left his family and riches behind and he never came back. Instead, he roamed the land in search of an answer to his question.

Many years later, he was sitting beneath a tree called a bodhi tree. He was thin and his clothes were in rags. But here he found his answer. He realized that people made themselves unhappy by wanting a comfortable life all the time. They didn't always understand that they could be peaceful and happy if they thought only about how to be good and how to do good things. So immediately Gautama set out to teach people his ideas. The teachings of Gautama spread through India and the rest of Asia. His followers called him the Buddha and his religion became one of the greatest in the world.

The **Buddha** discovered the secret of inner peace. This is why the statues of Buddha are always serene and smiling.

Terrors of the Tigris

The Assyrian came down like the wolf on the
fold,
And his cohorts were gleaming in purple and
gold.

This is how a poet imagined the cohorts or
armies of Assyrian soldiers as they attacked
the city of Babylon in 689 BC. They were a
terrifying sight. First came the chariots and
their drivers, led by the king himself –
Sennacherib. Then came the cavalry, armed
with bows and arrows. At the back marched
the foot soldiers, carrying long spears and
huge shields.

When he reached the walls, Sennacherib
shouted to the Babylonians to surrender. But
they refused. He became very angry and
ordered his army to attack. Bowmen fired
arrows at the defenders on the city walls.
Meanwhile, great wooden battering rams were
beaten against the gates. Then the Assyrians
poured in, burning the buildings and killing
all the people. The beautiful city was flattened
as if it had never existed.

The Assyrians, who came from the region
around the River Tigris, were some of the most
savage warriors the world has ever seen. Many
other armies were so frightened of them that
they gave in without a fight. In this way, the
kings of Assyria built up a vast empire in the
Middle East.

But Sennacherib did not live long to enjoy his triumphs. The Assyrian people were shocked at the destruction of Babylon, and began to plot against their king. And one day, when Sennacherib was praying in a temple, two of his own sons crept in and stabbed him to death.

Circles
of stone

The long line of men
pulled on their ropes.
They felt the massive stone
move a little further up the hill.
   The stone had been hauled for many
kilometres across southern England. Now that
it had reached the end of its journey, it had to
be tipped on end so it would stand upright.
A complete circle of these stones would be
formed, with other stones balanced on top.
   The great circle of stones took more than 600
years to finish, but by about 2,000 BC it was
complete. It is still standing today in southern
England. We call the circle Stonehenge.
   Stonehenge is one of the most mysterious of
all the buildings left behind by ancient people.
Why was it made? Certainly it was not a place
to live in or a storeroom, for it had no roof.
Some scientists believe it was a temple where

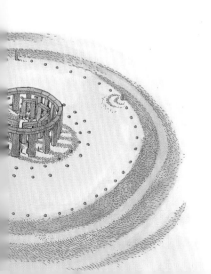

gods were worshipped. Others think it was built in honour of the sun.

A person standing in the middle of Stonehenge at dawn on the longest day of the year will see the sun rise exactly at the end of the path. This happens only on that one day. Stonehenge was almost certainly put where it is, and built the way it was, so that this would happen.

Some scientists believe it may have been a great deal more than a sun temple. They think it may actually have been what we would now call an observatory – a place for keeping track of the movements of the sun, moon and stars.

Bold sailors

Eight thousand years ago a small ship sailed from Phoenicia, a tiny country at the eastern end of the Mediterranean Sea. It was heading towards a little village on the coast of the land we now call Greece. The men on the ship were in high spirits. They had something very valuable, something that would make them all rich!

The little ship carried a load of shiny black stone – a stone we call obsidian. Obsidian was wanted by people throughout Greece. At that time all tools and weapons were made of stone. And obsidian was the best stone people

could get. It was easily chipped to make sharp knives, axes and spear-points.

But obsidian was hard to get. It came from the island of Melos, far to the south. A voyage to Melos was very dangerous. This made the obsidian very valuable. The Phoenicians were skilled sailors and would go on such dangerous journeys in search of wealth. This is how they became known as the first great traders.

Long ago, there was no such thing as money and people bartered or exchanged the things they wanted. Glass or pottery might be exchanged for oil or copper. A chunk of obsidian might be worth a basket of wheat or several fine animal skins. The sailors who had obsidian to trade could become wealthy.

The Phoenicians were bold and adventurous sailors. They sailed right across the Mediterranean and one of their expeditions went as far as Cornwall in England. Others are thought to have travelled right round Africa – a trip which took three years. And that's a long way to row!

The **Phoenicians** did not leave any drawings of their ships, but experts think their cargo ships looked like this.

China's Great Wall

How do you keep an enemy out of your land? One way is to build a high wall. This is just what the Chinese did, and because of its size, it turned out to be a very famous wall too.

Once there were many rulers in China. Those in the northern areas built short walls on their northern borders to keep out savage raiders. Later the whole of China was united under its first emperor. He ordered that some of the old walls should be joined up to form one new unbroken barrier stretching right across the country. When the work on these new sections was finished in 214 BC, it had taken less than twenty years to complete them. But hundreds of the labourers working on them died, either from enemy attacks or from the bitter cold.

The wall they left behind was more than two storeys high, and the top was wide enough for soldiers and horsemen to use it as a road. Watch-towers were built at certain points for extra protection.

In later years other emperors made repairs and added new sections to the Great Wall. The last work took place 400 years ago.

Much of the wall is still standing today. Following the land over mountains and valleys it measures about 4,800 kilometres. It's one of the great sights of the world – the longest wall ever built.

Giant heads

Here, surely, is the head of a giant! It's a face –
tall as an elephant! Its huge eyes are wide
open. On top it wears a strange kind of
helmet. And the whole thing is carved from a
single piece of stone.

There are at least fifteen of these huge heads.
They were found buried in the jungles of
Mexico. In the same area are more big statues,
in the shapes of jaguars and snakes. These
carvings are almost all that is left of some great
people we call the Olmecs. They lived
between 2,000 and 3,000 years ago.

The Olmecs knew nothing of the wheel.
They couldn't use metals. They didn't read or
write. But at the same time, all these things
were known about across the world in
Mesopotamia and Egypt. Thousands of
kilometres of ocean separated these
civilizations from the Olmecs.

Yet the Olmecs lasted for about 1,000 years.
We still know very little about the kind of
people they were. Much of what they made
has rotted away in the damp and heat of the
jungle. If only those giant heads could talk!

40

Greece and Rome

The Greeks discovered that the earth moved round the sun.

Greek citizens were all allowed to take part in government. They called it democracy. Many countries now use this system.

You probably enjoy the Olympic Games, trips to the theatre, studying maths and astronomy and perhaps you live in a centrally-heated house.

Over 2,000 years ago, the Greeks and Romans did the same things. They were the most advanced civilizations of that time. The citizens of Greece and Rome had time to think, to play and to build. Some of the results are part of our modern world.

Some of the plays they watched in the theatre are still performed today.

The laws of many modern countries are based on the ideas of Roman Law.

The Romans also had time to relax. They loved to watch gladiators fighting in the amphitheatre or to chat to their friends at the public baths.

At work they made a great contribution to the development of civilization. They were skilled builders. We still use some of their roads. Their laws are part of our modern laws.

The Romans ruled an empire of 60 million people. It needed great men like Julius Caesar to lead it and a mighty army to defend it against powerful enemies such as Hannibal. It was the greatest empire the world had seen.

Meeting at Olympia

All around the great arena the crowd watches excitedly. The runners crouch, ready for a race, and nearby, a javelin soars through the air.

Yes – this is a scene from a typical Olympic Games, which have developed from the Games held in Ancient Greece in 776 BC. Then, athletes from all over Greece travelled to Olympia to take part in the Games. There were no teams – each man competed just for himself. The event, called the pentathlon, included a sprint, discus and javelin throwing, a long jump and wrestling. The winners were not given medals, as they are today. They were presented with crowns made from olive leaves.

Olympic athletes were very famous in Ancient Greece. They were given huge banquets in their home towns, and statues of them were put up in city squares. Some were even excused from paying their taxes!

These early Olympics were held every four years. The Games were really a religious ceremony held in honour of Zeus, the king of the Greek gods. On the third day of the events, a great sacrifice was made to him.

Warriors of Sparta

The tall man picked up the baby. He felt its tiny arms and legs and saw how it screamed and kicked with rage. "Yes," he thought, "this child will make a fine warrior." He handed the baby back to its mother and went away. It was just as well that the baby was strong — weak children were left in the mountains to die or were thrown over a special cliff. You had to be tough to survive in Sparta!

Seven years later the tall man visited the child again. This time he took the boy away with him and the child never saw his family again. Instead he went to live with hundreds of other boys, and together they were taught how to fight.

All over Sparta boys were chosen and trained to be soldiers in this way. The Spartan army was the strongest in Greece. But it was a hard life. When the boys were twelve their underclothes were taken away and they were allowed only one outer garment a year. They were not allowed baths either, unless they wanted to wash in the river – which was icy cold in winter. Their food was plain and poor and there wasn't very much of it.

Sparta was a harsh place to live in. All kinds of luxuries such as fine food and clothes were forbidden. No one was rich. In fact it was against the law for Spartans to own gold or silver. We still use the word spartan today to describe someone who lives a very strict and simple life.

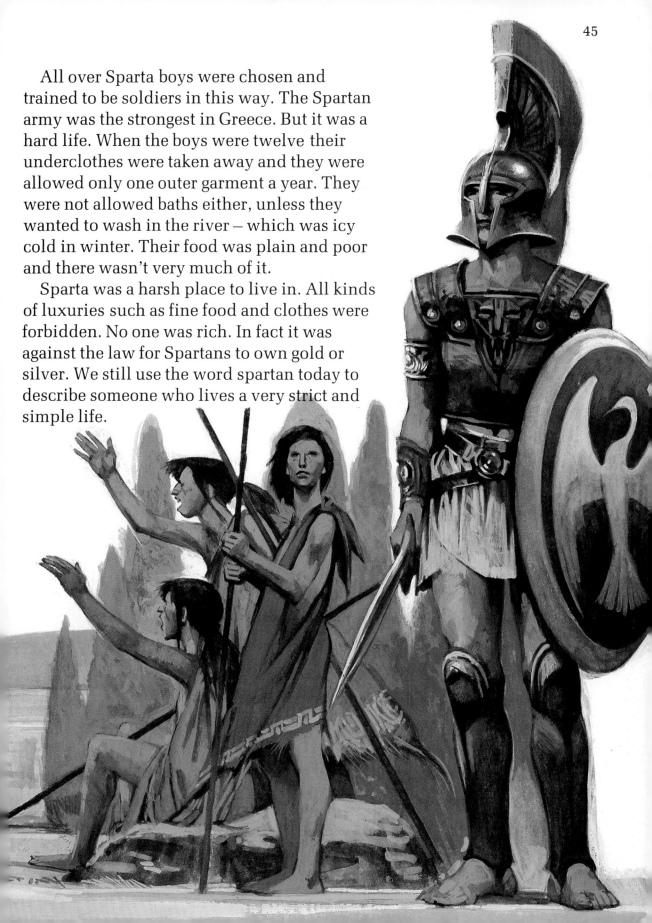

The wooden horse

Once, there was
a great city
called Troy.
It had high walls
and strong gates. For many years
the Greek army had been trying
to conquer this city, but they
could find no way in.

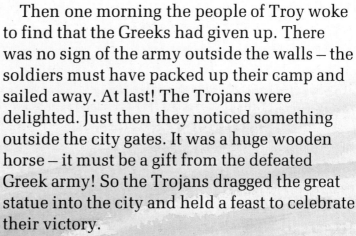

Then one morning the people of Troy woke to find that the Greeks had given up. There was no sign of the army outside the walls – the soldiers must have packed up their camp and sailed away. At last! The Trojans were delighted. Just then they noticed something outside the city gates. It was a huge wooden horse – it must be a gift from the defeated Greek army! So the Trojans dragged the great statue into the city and held a feast to celebrate their victory.

The Trojans slept well that night after all the merrymaking. But not everyone was asleep inside the city walls. There was a murmur and a scuffling which seemed to be coming from the belly of the wooden horse. Slowly a secret trap-door in the statue was gently pushed open, and one by one, a group of Greek soldiers crept out. They tiptoed to the city gates and opened them. The Greek army had only pretended to sail away. Now it had come back under cover of darkness. Once the gates were unlocked, the soldiers swept in, setting Troy on fire and killing people in their beds. The Trojans had been tricked – and Troy was burnt to the ground.

The tale of the Trojan War is one of the world's oldest stories. For hundreds of years, people believed it was true. But as time went on, people came to think it was only made up.

Today archaeologists are sure they have found Troy, buried under piles of earth and other ruins on the coast of Turkey. Most historians and archaeologists now believe that many old stories and legends are based, at least partly, on real places and on the true things that happened there.

Alexander and his horse

The great black horse kicked out wildly.
He reared and plunged. He would allow no
one near him.

King Philip of Macedon was furious at this. "The horse is mad!" he shouted. "A worthless beast! Take him away!" No wonder he was angry. He needed new war-horses for his army and this animal looked splendid. His name was Bucephalus and he was strong and beautiful. But if he was also bad-tempered, he would be no use to the army.

The king turned to go. Then suddenly his young son, Alexander ran forward. He stroked the horse's neck and spoke to him gently.

The young prince swung himself up on to the horse's back and galloped off. The pair seemed made for each other and King Philip was so delighted that he bought the horse as a present for his son.

And so Bucephalus became Alexander's war-horse. Together they rode into many battles. When his father died, Alexander became king of Macedon and set out to build up a huge empire. Riding his favourite horse, he led his army as far as Egypt and then India. Bucephalus died in India in 326 BC. Alexander buried him and founded a new city called Bucephalus in honour of his beloved horse.

The rise of Rome

Once upon a time, in Italy, there were twin boys called Romulus and Remus. Their uncle was a wicked man and wanted to get rid of them. He ordered the babies to be thrown into the River Tiber. But first their mother placed them in a basket, hoping that somehow it would help save their lives.

The river was in flood and the boys were washed ashore, alive and well in their little basket. A she-wolf found them first, and gave them milk, just as if they were cubs. Then the king's shepherd, Faustulus, discovered them and took them to his home to care for them. When the boys grew up, they returned to their uncle's land and built a new city. That city was Rome.

The story of Romulus and Remus is a legend, but the city of Rome is real. The place where the city stands used to be an easy

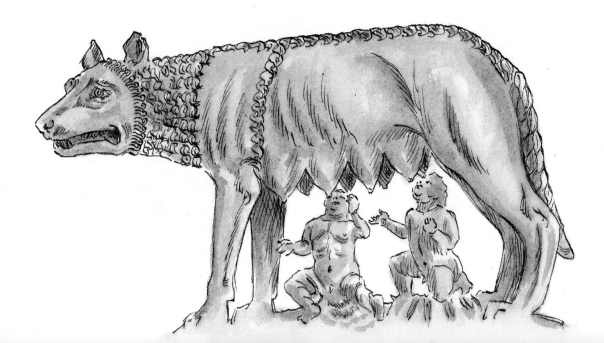

crossing point on the River Tiber. In the early
days, two villages existed there. But in about
575 BC nearby marshy ground was drained
while the Great Sewer was built. The level
ground was then paved and it became a good
place for meetings and trade. From this
beginning, the city grew and grew.

By 250 BC Rome was the most powerful city
in all Italy. Its soldiers were well trained and
heavily armed, and they were proud of their
city. The Romans used to meet in open spaces
called forums. The most important of these
was the Forum Romanum, and it was filled
with beautiful halls, temples and arches,
where people could walk together and discuss
things – or simply stroll alone and think. The
main street of Rome, called the Sacred Way,
crossed the Forum Romanum. The Sacred Way
seemed the very heart of Rome at its most
powerful – proud and wealthy Romans strode
about there, and victorious generals marched
their armies down this street in triumph.

Elephants in the Alps

High up in the Alps, the line of elephants trudged slowly through the snow. Their huge feet slipped and slithered on the icy track. It was a long way from the sunny lands they were used to!

But what were they doing there? It was 217 BC and an army general called Hannibal had brought the elephants, along with his soldiers, into the mountains as part of his bold plan to conquer all Italy. His country, called Carthage, had been at war with Rome for many years, and now Hannibal was determined to

capture the great Italian city. Some of the
elephants carried the baggage needed for
Hannibal's army, and the biggest elephant of
all carried Hannibal himself. Few Romans had
ever seen such huge animals before, and
Hannibal hoped they would be terrified.

But Hannibal's plan didn't quite work out.
Most of the elephants died while crossing the
Alps, and those that were left soon died in
Italy. Hannibal nearly captured Rome and he
beat the Roman army in three great battles. But
then he ran short of soldiers and food and
returned to Carthage. His magnificent plan had
failed.

Joining the army

The boy stands blinking in the bright sunlight. He shifts his shoulders backwards and forwards, feeling the weight of his new armour. The man who's been fitting the armour looks at the new recruit and frowns.

"Hold still!" he grumbles as he reaches up to try a helmet on the young boy's head. "There! All you need now is a shield and you'll be ready to take your place with the others."

Wearing armour is just one of the things that this boy must get used to. At the age of sixteen, he's just joined the Roman army as a foot-soldier. Now he lives away from home, at a camp where he will learn how to fight.

When they arrived at the camp, the new recruits had to make a promise to be loyal to the emperor. Then they were fitted with a uniform. All the soldiers wore a tunic underneath armour which was made of leather and metal. Their helmets were made of heavy bronze, lined with leather.

The training sessions 2,000 years ago were long and hard. Twice a day the young soldiers had to march along carrying a large shield in one hand and a long spear in the other. They learned to fight by using wooden swords in mock battles with the other boys. They even had to learn to swim across rivers wearing their armour.

When the boys finished their training, they were sent out to march with the main army. They helped to build and protect the huge Roman Empire which had now spread across Europe and North Africa. Some of the long, straight roads that the soldiers built as they marched can still be seen today.

We who are about to die

The fighters stride into the arena. A great roar goes up from the 50,000 people watching. Then all is suddenly quiet again as the fighters turn to the emperor who is sitting in the royal box. "We who are about to die salute you!" they shout.

Now the battle begins. The fighters, called gladiators, face each other in pairs. Some use swords and shields. Others hold three-pronged spears and nets. They know it's a fight to the death. But if a beaten gladiator puts up a really good fight, the crowd may wave their handkerchiefs. This means that they want the man to live.

The Romans loved to go to these combats. They were held in a place called the Colosseum in Rome, a building about as big as a modern football stadium. Many of the contests were wild and dramatic. At one time, the arena was flooded so that battles between ships could be fought. Later, cages underneath the stadium were filled with hungry animals, which were let out to fight the gladiators.

The **Colosseum** still stands today, but much of it is in ruins. The gladiators and wild animals are gone, of course. Only tourists and guides – and plenty of stray cats – are left.

Death on the cross

"Kill Jesus! Kill Jesus!"

The crowd shouted and waved their sticks. In the middle of all the people was a boy called Malchus who had come with his master, the Chief Priest of the Temple. They were going to arrest a man who had been causing trouble in the city. The man's name was Jesus, and he called himself the Son of God.

The shouts grew louder. But Malchus watched Jesus standing quietly in front of the crowd. Suddenly there was a struggle. Some men seized Jesus. One of Jesus's friends tried to save him. He drew his sword and swung it about wildly. Poor Malchus! The blade hit him! He cried out in pain and fell to the ground. Blood poured from his ear.

Jesus didn't try to fight. He calmly turned to his friend and said, "Put away your sword. I am not afraid." He bent down to Malchus and touched his ear gently. At once the pain seemed to disappear. Then the crowd caught hold of Jesus again and led him away.

The next day, Jesus was put to death on a cross. But he was not forgotten. His followers believed he was God's son and that he came to life again. They began to travel to other lands, telling everyone about this miracle, and teaching them that people should love one another. What they said gave hope to thousands of people. In this way the teachings of Jesus Christ were spread far and wide. A new religion, called Christianity, had begun.

Jesus was put to death on a wooden cross. This sculpture at a shrine in Portugal shows him carrying the cross to the place where he died.

An emperor's dream

Long ago, in AD 312, a Roman leader called Constantine had to fight a battle to become emperor. The night before his army was due to fight, he claimed he had a strange dream. In this dream he saw a huge cross in the sky. And on the cross were the words, 'Conquer with this sign'.

What could this mean? Constantine remembered that the cross was the sign of Jesus Christ. Jesus had been killed on a cross and many people believed he had come to life again. They followed a religion called Christianity, which Jesus had started.

Constantine decided to take notice of his dream. He ordered his soldiers to paint the first two letters of the Greek word for Christ on their shields. And, carrying these, they went on to win the battle. Constantine was grateful, and he did a great deal to help other Christians. He gave them money to build

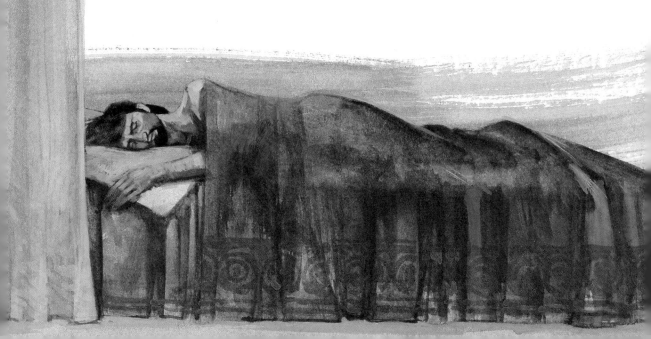

churches, and he ordered his soldiers to go to
church parades. In AD 320 he made
Christianity the state religion.

Then Constantine moved out of Rome to
build a new capital in the east. He went to a
town on the Black Sea, called Byzantium.
He rebuilt the town into a beautiful city which
he called Constantinople, and which was to
become the centre of Christianity. Today, we
call this city Istanbul.

The Middle Ages

Roman roads, buildings and waterways fell into ruin, and the people were afraid. In time, the emperor Charlemagne restored some order and protection, but his empire failed too during the ninth century.

Now the people found a new way to organize themselves. It was called the feudal system. The lords were given lands by the king, in return for their service and loyalty.

The peasants were given land to farm and protection from raiders in return for working for the local lord.

During the fourth century, the mighty Roman Empire had stretched from the north of England to the Red Sea in the East. But by the fifth century, the power of the empire had begun to dwindle. The Romans returned to Italy, leaving the countries of Europe open to attack from barbarian tribes such as the Goths and Vandals.

Elsewhere in the world, civilization was still flourishing. Marco Polo found a rich and wonderful empire when he visited China. Before then, hardly anyone had travelled between Europe and the East, but more and more people began to follow his route across the world to trade goods.

Unfortunately, goods were not the only thing brought back from Asia. In the fourteenth century Europe was hit by a terrible plague called the Black Death.

The spread of religion also united people. Christianity brought Europe together. Islam united the peoples of the Middle East and North Africa. Sadly, religion also caused wars. Christians and Muslims fought each other, because each side believed that theirs was the only true religion.

Barbarian attack

"Kill the barbarians!" shouted the Roman soldiers.

"They're stupid!"

"They're ugly and hairy!"

The Romans laughed at the wild, bearded soldiers running to attack them.

But the Romans didn't laugh for long, for these barbarians were fierce fighters. They rushed at the Roman army, shouting in their strange language and waving their clubs and axes. They pushed the Romans back and killed many of them.

The Romans thought that anyone who lived outside the Roman Empire was a barbarian, and they did their best to protect their lands against them. But as the Roman army grew weaker, the barbarians grew stronger.

One tribe, the Goths, lived in what is now Germany. They fought their way across the borders of the Empire many times. In AD 410, an army of Goths even broke into the city of Rome itself. And again in AD 476, more barbarians invaded the whole of Italy, getting rid of the last Roman emperor. The great age of Roman rule was at an end – and it was the 'stupid' barbarians who had destroyed it.

A visit from the Vikings

Thick, white fog drifted over the North Sea and the coast of England. Only the screeches of gulls and the hiss of waves rolling up on the shore broke the silence. Suddenly a new sound could be heard – it was the swish of oars. A fleet of long warships came sliding through the fog like thin, grey ghosts. The ships were carved and painted to look like dragons, and they were full of fierce warriors from the Northland, the area we now call Scandinavia. The year was AD 789, and the Vikings had arrived to attack Britain.

For a long time after this, the British suffered terribly from the raids of the Vikings. The

raiders sailed quietly along the coast, or up a river, to some unsuspecting town. Then the warriors swarmed ashore to burn down the buildings and carry off all the treasure they could find. They also took people with them, to be used as slaves.

Many of the Vikings joined together to form big armies. They conquered large parts of Britain and settled on the land. Because of their well-built longships and their skills as seamen, the Vikings were able to attack many other lands too. They sailed far away from their homeland – to Spain, Italy and Morocco. They explored France by sailing up the rivers, and they travelled to the Mediterranean Sea and conquered Sicily.

Island of the Princes

King Alfred stood on top of the hill and looked about him. All around he could see nothing but marshes and woods. His hill was really a little island high above the floods. Alfred decided this was just the place to hide. No one could get to the island without being seen. There were trees to shelter in and plenty of deer to hunt for food. He'd be safe here with his soldiers until he was ready to fight.

Alfred had become King of Wessex, one of the seven kingdoms of England, in AD 871, and he soon started to fight against the Danes. For many years the Danish army had been roaming the land, robbing and killing, but by this time they had settled down in some parts of England, especially in the east and north. The whole of England might soon be in the power of the Danes.

All through the long, hard winter and the early spring, Alfred waited patiently.
He gathered a new, strong army of local men. At last they were ready! Early in May in AD 878, Alfred's army marched eastwards, collecting more men as it went along. And after a great battle, the Danes were defeated. The Danish leader, Guthrum, signed an agreement with Alfred, and the two kings divided the country between them. Alfred and Guthrum were soon friends and Guthrum became a Christian.

But this was not the end of the fighting. Alfred went on to capture London from the Danes, and he built strongholds and a good navy to defend his lands against future attacks. But he didn't forget his hiding place in the marshes. A splendid abbey was built there, and it was named Athelney – Island of the Princes.

Followers of the **Islamic** religion are called **Muslims**. Today thousands of Muslims from all over the world flock to **Mecca** – just as they have done for hundreds of years.

Flight to Medina

In AD 622 a band of men and women set out from the city of Mecca in Arabia. Their leader was called Muhammad. He was a rich man, but he was leaving most of his wealth behind.

Muhammad had angered the people of Mecca, and now he was running for his life! For Muhammad believed there was only one God, called Allah, and everyone should worship him. He'd had messages from God, and now Muhammad was trying to spread the word. But the people of Mecca liked to worship many different gods – they also liked the trade that was brought into their city by the pilgrims who came to worship these many gods. Only a few people listened to what Muhammad was saying.

Muhammad and his followers travelled a long way until they found a safe place to live and preach. At last they were made welcome in the town of Yathrib. Here Muhammad began to organize a new kind of religion, called Islam. Muhammad himself was called the Prophet, and he gave the town a new name too – Medina, which means The City (of the Prophet).

The message of Islam spread quickly through Arabia. People wanted the mercy and justice that this new religion spoke of, and soon Muhammad had a powerful army. Eight years after he'd run away, Muhammad was able to return in triumph to Mecca. He went straight to the shrine in the main square and tore down the statues of the gods.

Muhammad died at the age of sixty-two, but his new religion lived on. His messages from Allah were collected together in a holy book called the Koran. Muhammad's followers soon controlled the whole of Arabia. Arab armies surged northwards and westwards, carrying the banner of Islam to many other lands.

Muslims wait their turn to enter the **Great Mosque** at Medina. Within its walls is the sacred shrine of the Islamic religion.

The warrior scholar

King Charlemagne had a secret. He couldn't write. He tried very hard to learn, and every night he placed a pen and paper by his bed so that he could practise. Every time he rode out to war, the pen and paper went with him, but he still couldn't write.

As a little boy, Charlemagne had been brought up in the court of his father, Pepin. Pepin was king of the Franks, the people who lived in the land we now call France. Pepin's main aim in life was to drive back the Arab armies, which had threatened to spread right across Europe. So Charlemagne's early years had been spent in learning to fight and he'd had no time to study. He defeated the Arabs in France with his father, and then in AD 771 he became king of the Franks himself. He grew up to be a tall, strong and handsome man who was feared by his enemies.

Charlemagne was a very powerful king. He had protected Christian Europe from the Arab invasion and in AD 800 he was created holy emperor of that region. He was an intelligent leader too. He loved talking with poets and artists, and listening to scholars. His court at Aachen, in present-day Germany, became a centre of learning. Charlemagne set up schools throughout his kingdom, so that children could learn to count, to read and to write.

Kings, knights and peasants

6
The lords served the king and provided him with knights for his army.

1
The **king** gave estates to the church and the lords.

2
The **lords** gave land to the knights.

In the medieval feudal system, the king ruled all the land and everyone served him. The king gave large areas of land, or estates, to the church and to the lords, his richest and most loyal followers.

The bishops and the lords then gave pieces of their estates to the knights. And the knights

5

The knights protected the lords.

gave smaller pieces of their land to the peasants.

In return for the use of this land, the peasants worked several days each week for the knights. The knights had to protect and serve the lords, and the lords had to serve the king, providing him with knights in time of war. So every person except the king had a duty to serve someone else.

4

In return, the **peasants** worked for the knights.

3

The **knights** gave farms to the peasants.

A present from the enemy

In 1192, King Richard of England galloped into battle. He was a big, strong man and he waved a huge sword bravely in front of him as he dashed along. His enemies were terrified. They ran back across the dusty plain as he came near.

Suddenly the king's horse was hit by an arrow! The great animal crashed to the ground, and Richard was pulled down with it into the dirt. His men helped him up and took him to his tent, but he could not rest. He must lead his army. He had to get another horse and go back to the fighting. But where could he find one strong enough to carry him?

Just then a servant came to Richard's tent. He brought with him two magnificent war-horses. "Sire," he said, "these are a present from Saladin. He saw you fall and he has sent you new horses to ride."

King Richard was amazed. Saladin was the leader of the enemy. He was a Muslim, a follower of the religion called Islam. And King Richard was a Christian. He'd come to the East to drive the Muslims out of the Holy Land of Israel, in one of the religious wars called the Crusades. Yet here was his enemy sending him a present!

King Richard didn't stand about thinking for long. He jumped on to one of the new horses and rode back into the battle. Both armies fought hard, and the Christians won. But Richard was never able to defeat Saladin completely, and most of the Holy Land stayed in the hands of the Muslims for many years.

The name **Crusades** comes from the old French word 'cruz' meaning cross. King Richard's men wore a red cross as a badge, because they were fighting for Christianity.

Pilgrims on the road

"I can see it!" shouted the man excitedly. He pointed ahead, and the others behind him peered into the distance. Then they saw it too. Far away, they could just make out a group of buildings – at last, it was the town they had travelled such a long way to see!

The town was called Santiago, which means the city of Saint James. Santiago was the Spanish city where the body of Saint James was buried, and the travellers had come all the way from England to see the Saint's church. It was a very important place for Christians.

These travellers were called pilgrims. Some were rich and some were poor. Some rode on horseback, but most walked, leaning on heavy wooden sticks called staffs. They wore robes of shaggy wool. Many had no shoes, but they seemed happy as they went along – they sang songs and rang little bells. Whenever they came to a city, they marched through the streets and the townspeople came out to cheer them.

During the Middle Ages, thousands of pilgrims made these long journeys to holy places everywhere. Christians went to Rome or Jerusalem and other places that were important in their religion. Muslims, the followers of the religion called Islam, went to Mecca in Arabia. The pilgrims' journeys were often long and dangerous, but they went to show their love and respect for God, and to say sorry for the wrongs they had done. And they hoped God would bless them.

The very mighty lord

In 1206 the Mongolian leader Temujin wanted just one thing. He wanted to conquer the whole world! So his chieftains gave him a new name – Genghis Khan – which means Universal Ruler or Ruler of the World.

The name soon struck terror into many hearts. From the grassy plains of Mongolia in central Asia, Genghis Khan set out on his conquests. His soldiers were tough and well-trained, and they lived on a diet of dried meat and mare's milk, which they believed kept them strong.

They had a trick when they rode into battle – they kept as quiet as possible, so the only sound was the horses' hoofs thudding on the grass. This would terrify the enemy, who were used to hearing noisy battle cries. The Mongolian horsemen could control their horses with their feet only, and this left both hands free to fire their bows and arrows.

First of all Genghis Khan invaded China, and his soldiers broke through the Great Wall. When they had defeated the Chinese army, the soldiers went on to destroy towns and villages. They burned buildings and killed millions of people. In a few years, the north of China was a wilderness.

Then Genghis Khan turned to the west. The Mongols swept across Asia into what is now Iran. They left behind a trail of ruined cities and beaten armies, and people fled in fear as they approached. Russia was invaded too. The Mongolian army went on to reach the edge of Europe. But in 1227, Genghis Khan died, and his body was carried back to the plains of Mongolia to be buried. He hadn't succeeded in conquering the world, but he had built the biggest empire in history.

The wonderful tales of Marco Polo

In 1295, three travellers arrived in Venice, in Italy. They were dressed in threadbare clothes and they spoke in a strange language. Nobody recognized them, but they said that Venice was their home – even though they'd almost forgotten how to speak Italian.

The men had been away for twenty-four years! Their family had given them up for dead. One of the travellers had been a young man of seventeen when he'd left – now he was a middle-aged man of forty-one. His name was Marco Polo.

Marco Polo was full of stories about the wonderful things he'd seen in China. The Chinese, he explained, did not write out their books by hand – instead they printed many of them at a time. They used clocks which were powered by water. They made colourful fireworks from a strange thing called gunpowder.

At that time, no one in Italy had ever heard of gunpowder, or printing, or clocks. People found it hard to believe Marco Polo – they thought he was either making it up, or that all three men were mad. Suddenly Marco Polo took hold of his clothes and ripped them open – and out tumbled a pile of diamonds, rubies, pearls and other precious stones! At the sight of these riches, everyone realized that the travellers had really been on a marvellous journey, and that all Marco Polo's wonderful tales were true.

The Black Death

In 1347 a fleet of ships arrived at a port called
Messina, in Sicily. Everyone on board was
dead or dying. Their skin was covered in dark
blotches and their bodies were swollen. What
was this mysterious illness? Nobody in
Messina knew, but soon they were catching it
too. Thousands of citizens died in the next few

weeks, and the terrified people drove the ships out of port. But it was too late.

The disease was called the Black Death. It quickly spread across Sicily and into Italy. Then for four years it raged through Europe, killing millions of people – about a quarter of all the people who lived there! Everyone was afraid, because there was no way of curing it. Some even thought that the end of the world had come. People flocked to the churches and prayed. They wore good luck charms for protection, and they mixed all kinds of herbs together to make medicines. Nothing helped.

Where had the Black Death started? It probably began in Asia and moved west. The germs were carried by the fleas living on the black rats on board cargo ships. When the ships sailed to another country, the rats went with them, and so the awful disease was taken across a large part of the world.

After the Black Death, there was still work to be done but fewer people to do it. A good worker could choose who he worked for, instead of belonging to one master. This meant that the feudal lords had less power over their workers.

Spreading culture

Today the world seems a small and familiar place. You can eat hamburgers in New York and Melbourne, drive the same car in London and Tokyo, wear tee shirts in Paris and Buenos Aires.

500 years ago it was different. People did not travel and knew little about the world. Many thought the world was flat and if you sailed too far west you would fall off the end.

Knowledge was also being spread. Gutenberg's printing press, invented in 1454, helped the spread of ideas. There was a renewed interest in learning, especially about the ancient worlds of Greece and Rome.

Gutenberg's press

Mayan civilization

Mali civilization

People had never heard of great civilizations like Mali in West Africa or the Maya in Central America.

This ignorance was about to change. Advances in ship-building and navigation made longer voyages possible.

Artists were encouraged and some like Michelangelo and Leonardo da Vinci produced many fine works. They were supported by the rich merchants in cities such as Venice and Florence.

This revival of learning also led to the formation of the Protestant Church. Luther nailed his criticisms of the Roman Church to a church door in Wittenberg, and split the Catholic Church. The old beliefs and views were under fire.

Settlers like the Portuguese missionaries took their culture to other countries. In 1557 they settled on the coast of China in a place we now call Macao.

In 1492 Columbus discovered the route to America and in 1522, after a three-year voyage, Magellan's expedition proved the world was round. All the unknown oceans had been crossed. Our modern world was taking shape.

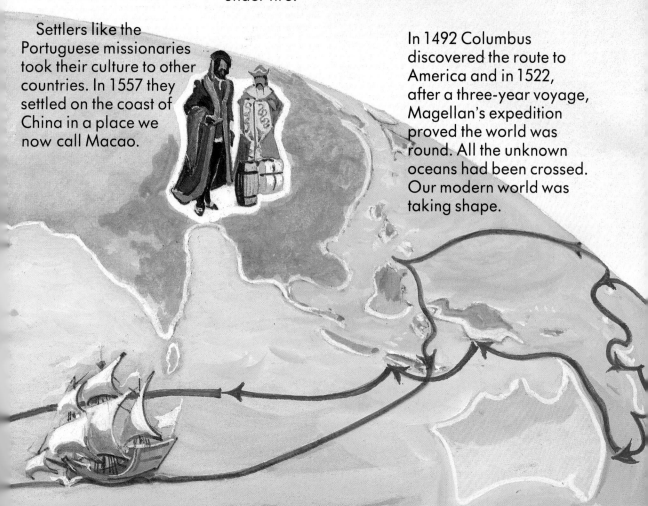

Explorers ventured further in search of trade and wealth. Bartholomew Diaz found the way round the tip of Africa to the spice trade across the Indian Ocean.

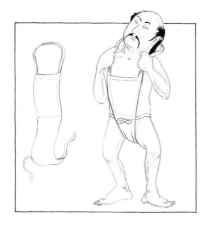

Shoguns means no guns!

Here is a man getting dressed. First he puts on a vest, then a gown and then a pair of baggy shorts. Next he puts on shoes and shin-guards, then pieces of armour which cover his shoulders, his back and his waist. A mask and helmet covers the face, and last of all he straps on two swords – a long, curved one and a short, thick one with a vicious point.

This man is a warrior called a samurai. He lived in Japan 300 years ago. The samurai were some of the most respected people in Japan, and they were proud and ferocious fighters.

But why doesn't this samurai carry a gun? After all, soldiers in many other countries were using guns at this time. Swords are not much use against bullets and cannon-balls. The answer is that guns were forbidden. The Japanese leaders, called shoguns, thought that firearms were evil, so they banned them. All the guns in the country were locked up in storerooms, and bows and spears were not allowed to be used either. The samurai were the only people in the country who were allowed to have any weapons and they ruled supreme.

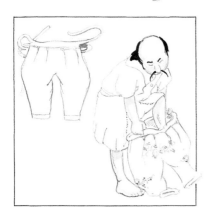

The shoguns banned many other things too. They wanted to stop Japan being influenced by other countries. So they either killed or sent home all foreigners. They stopped trading with most European countries, and they stopped any Japanese person from going abroad. Anyone who disobeyed the rules was put to death.

A Mayan ball game

What kind of game is this? There are two teams, with three players on each side. They are wearing gloves and pads and they are hitting a bouncy rubber ball at each other. But they mustn't touch the ball with their hands — instead, they use their wrists, elbows and ankles.

The game is being played in a huge yard with two sloping walls. High up on one wall is a small stone ring. The players are trying to knock the ball through the ring. If they do this, they'll win the game.

It sounds a bit like the game of basketball that we play today. But this game was played over 800 years ago by the Maya people, who lived in what is now Mexico, in Central America. The Maya built ball courts in many of their cities. To them the game was not just a sport, it was part of a religious ceremony. It told the story of the fight between good and evil. It might have been a display in honour of the gods, asking for a good harvest.

We aren't sure today exactly why the game was played, but we can say that it was probably very difficult to get the ball through the tiny ring. And it was even harder for the team that lost, since they might end up being killed as a sacrifice to the gods. On the other hand, anyone who scored a goal might be allowed to take all the jewellery and clothes from the people who were watching!

Empire in the sand

Trumpets blared, drums rolled and out on to the platform stepped a magnificent figure. He wore a golden cap and a bright, velvet cloak. On his shoulder he carried a bow. Behind him, there were rows and rows of slaves – 300 altogether – and they were all armed. In front of him, musicians played two-stringed guitars made of gold and silver.

This is how the great leader Mansa Musa looked to foreign travellers, over 600 years ago. Mansa Musa was one of the kings who ruled an empire stretching for 1,600 kilometres across western Africa. It was the kingdom of Mali. Although much of it was desert, it was still a very rich land. The wealth came from one thing – gold.

The kings of Mali ruled in the fourteenth
century. At that time, people from other
countries knew very little about Africa. Those
who did visit Mali were amazed – it was
splendid! The cities were full of fine buildings
hung with silk curtains. Copper statues
decorated the streets. The people of Mali used
coins made from solid gold, and the king
himself was said to own 10,000 horses.
Travellers were just as amazed by the manners
of the people there. In Mali there were no
thieves and hardly any crimes. Foreigners
were made welcome wherever they went.
It seemed to be a charmed empire in the sand.

The terrors of the Bulging Cape

"Your Highness, the sailors are afraid! They will not sail round the Cape. They say that there the sea boils and turns red, that there are sandbanks and whirlpools. They think it's the edge of the world!"

Prince Henry of Portugal often heard stories like this from his sea-captains. He sent many ships out to find a way round Africa, but they never got further than the place they called the Bulging Cape. There the crews became so afraid that they turned round and sailed home.

The year was 1433. At that time, very little of the world had been explored and nobody in Europe knew how big Africa was. No one was even certain whether the earth itself was flat or round. Perhaps if a ship sailed too far to the south it might fall off the edge of the world!

But Prince Henry was determined to find out the truth. He wanted to trade with West Africa, to get some of the precious gold and ivory he knew was there. He also needed to find another way to the Far East where spices came from, because his overland route had been cut off by the Turks. At last one of the captains got round the Bulging Cape. He reported that the coast of Africa went on to the south for as far as he could see.

After this, many more ships followed. Each one went a little further than the last. But another fifty-five years passed before Bartholomew Diaz went round the southernmost tip of the huge continent. He called it the Cape of Good Hope.

Across the Pacific

Imagine you live on a small island. It is getting crowded with people, and you want to find a new home where there is more room. So what do you do? You get into a boat and set off to find another island.

This is just what the first sailors in the Pacific Ocean did. The Pacific is the biggest stretch of water in the world and dotted about the ocean are thousands of small islands. Some lie near each other in groups, but between others there may be huge distances of empty sea.

The very first sailors probably started from somewhere in South-East Asia. More than 3,000 years ago they reached the islands of Tonga and Samoa. Then they spread out to find homes in all the other islands of the Pacific. Today we call these sailors Polynesians.

A Polynesian boat was made by lashing two canoes side by side with a space in between. A deck was built over the space to carry passengers and food, with a small hut for shelter. These double canoes were moved by paddles, but they also had sails made of woven leaves. A boat like this could hold as many as fifty people, along with pigs and other animals. The people also took fruit and vegetables to plant in their new home.

Around the world

Have you ever been hungry? Really hungry?

Imagine you are on board a sailing ship in the middle of a huge ocean. The only food left is some biscuits, but these are stale and rotten. The drinking water is so old it has gone yellow. You get so hungry that you eat anything you can get – sawdust from the floor – even rats!

This is what happened to a band of explorers from Spain who set sail in September 1519 in five ships. There was a crew of 234 men, but they were not told where they were going. They would be crossing an ocean but no one knew how big it was. Nobody from Europe had ever been there before. And they didn't know what they would find on the other side.

The leader of the crew, Ferdinand Magellan, had a bold plan. He wanted to reach the Spice Islands where precious spices could be bought. But instead of sailing to the east, he decided to go west. If the earth was round, as some people said, surely he would get there just as easily by sailing round the tip of South America?

The voyage was a dreadful one. First the men rebelled against the captain in a mutiny, then one of the ships sank. And then came the terrible crossing of the unknown ocean, during which nineteen men died. But instead of sailing right round South America, they discovered the short-cut we now call the Strait of Magellan. At last they reached more peaceful waters. They called these waters the

Pacific Ocean, after the Portuguese word for peace.

But another disaster happened when Magellan was killed in a battle in the Philippines. In the end only one ship and eighteen men got all the way home to Spain, arriving in September 1522. They were the first people to sail right round the world. And they had proved at last that the earth was round.

The room full of gold

It doesn't sound like a fair fight. On one side, thousands of warriors. On the other, just 180 Spanish soldiers. But the soldiers won.

They had come all the way to Peru in South America to find treasure, in 1532. They were greedy for gold and nothing would stop them. Besides, they had guns and horses. The people of Peru, called Incas, had never seen these things before. They were terrified and ran away.

Pizarro, the leader of the Spaniards, was amazed at his victory. Not one of his soldiers had been killed. The Inca king, called Atahualpa, had been captured and put in prison. Now came the job of gathering together all the treasure. It would take a long time.

Pizarro came to like Atahualpa and promised he wouldn't kill him. In return, Atahualpa said, "If you set me free, I will fill this room with gold. And I will fill another room twice over with silver." Pizarro accepted this offer and the gold and silver began to pour in. But before the rooms were full, Pizarro changed his mind. He knew that if he let the king go he'd have trouble on his hands – the Inca warriors might attack. So he gave orders for Atahualpa to be killed.

During the next six years the Spaniards stripped the Incas of nearly all their wealth. A great empire was destroyed by a handful of armed men.

The pioneer of printing

It was a miracle!

The priest stared at the paper. The writing on it was clear and there wasn't a single mistake. He looked at the next sheet. And the next. They were all just as good.

"Who did this beautiful writing?" he asked. Johann Gutenberg laughed. "It wasn't written by anyone," he replied.

The priest looked even more baffled. He had asked Gutenberg to make some copies of a

church document. At this time, over 500 years ago, everything was copied out by hand. Clerks sat all day at their desks, writing out books and documents with pen and ink. Yet this man was saying that his copies had been made by no one. He must be a magician.

But Gutenberg was not a magician. He was a printer from Mainz in Germany, and he had invented a way of making copies with a machine called a printing press. Each page was set out in blocks of raised letters, called type. Ink was painted on to the blocks, and the sheets of paper were pressed over them. When enough copies of a page had been made, the type could be moved about to form new words, and so used over and over again. The first book printed by Gutenberg in this way was a Latin Bible, in 1454.

It's no wonder the priest was amazed. Gutenberg's press could produce about 300 sheets a day – many, many more than even the speediest clerk could ever hope to finish by hand. Until that time there had been very few books in the world. The invention of the printing press meant that thousands could be made in a short time, and so they became cheaper. In this way, new ideas and learning could be spread faster than ever before.

A marvel in marble

Michelangelo looked at the huge block of marble. He ran his hands over it – how cold and smooth it felt. What would he make from it?

The people of Florence in Italy had asked him to carve them a statue. They knew he was the greatest sculptor in the land and they would pay him well.

Michelangelo set to work. He hated to be watched, so a tall screen was put up around the block while he chipped away. Day after day he worked, all alone. No one was allowed to look.

At last, after two years, the statue was nearly ready. One of the leaders of Florence asked if he could inspect it, so Michelangelo let him come behind the screen. The man stared in wonder at the massive figure that had been carved from the marble. It was magnificent! But he thought he should make a comment. "I think the nose is a little thick," he said.

Michelangelo didn't reply. Instead he picked up his tools and climbed up to the statue's head. Hidden in his left hand was some marble dust. As he pretended to chip away at the nose, he let the dust fall from his hand. The man was fooled by this. "It's much better now!" he called.

Michelangelo's statue, called David, was finished in 1504. It was carved from a single block of marble, four metres tall, and can still be seen in Florence today.

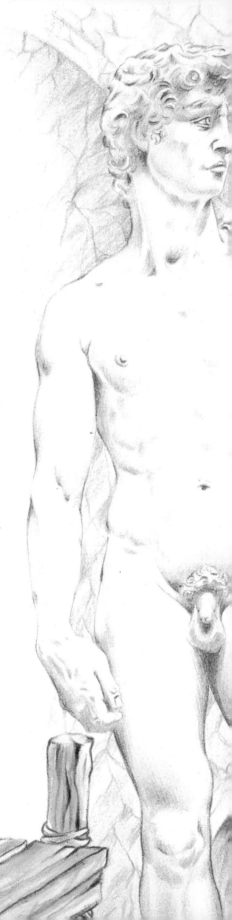

In the sixteenth century, the rich merchants used their wealth to pay artists to work for them. Fine painting and sculpture appeared in all the big European cities, and artists such as Michelangelo were looked upon as important people. Their works of art told the story of the cities' greatness.

Religious rebel

Bang! Bang! Bang!

The hammer blows echoed on the church door. But Martin Luther was glad of the noise. He was nailing up a big piece of paper – and he wanted everyone to know about it.

It was 1517 in Wittenberg in Germany, and Martin Luther was angry. He had become upset with the priests of the Catholic religion, whose leader was the Pope in Rome. Luther thought they'd grown lazy and too fond of money. One thing that especially annoyed him was the way they charged people money for forgiving their sins. Luther thought the Catholic priests were forgetting the teachings of the Bible.

So Martin Luther wrote down a list of all his complaints – there were ninety-five of them! Then he nailed the list to the church door. The townsfolk came to read it, and many agreed that Luther was right. Copies of the list were sent all round Germany, and soon Luther had hundreds of people to support him.

This was the beginning of a new kind of Christianity. Its followers were called Protestants, because they agreed with Martin Luther's protests. There were soon other religious movements of protest in Europe, following on from Luther – there were the followers of Calvin in France and Switzerland and of a man called Knox in Scotland. The new teachings looked at the Bible as a model, and they soon spread throughout Europe. Services were given in people's native language instead of Latin, which the locals couldn't understand. The new teachings caused many arguments – some of which were so fierce that they ended in wars – but the Protestants were at last allowed to worship as they wanted.

The king who played at soldiers

Prince Peter liked playing at soldiers with his friends. He was always the leader, of course. He was a big boy and rather a bully. And everyone had to do what he told them. They knew that one day he'd be King of Russia, the biggest country in the world.

Peter took his games very seriously and organized his friends into different armies. Because he was a prince, he was given real guns to use! The prince didn't have to make his own forts out of boxes, or even use toy ones. He had a real castle built for him so he could practise attacking and defending it. And rowing boats were turned into little warships so that he and his friends could fight mock sea battles on a lake.

Peter became King of Russia in 1696. He had grown into a giant of a man, but he hadn't forgotten his soldier games. He built up a new Russian navy, using the best European engineers and scientists he could find to work on a new fleet of ships. Then he organized a professional army for Russia. With the new army and navy he added even more land to his kingdom, and made sure his lands were well protected.

King Peter wanted to make Russia a modern country. Up until this time it had not kept up with the rest of Europe. Peter learned as much as he could from the West, and was

determined to use his knowledge to change Russia for the better. He believed education was very important and he wanted his people to be well educated. So he set up high schools, and at one time he tried to force all young noblemen to go to school by allowing no man to marry until he could read and write.

King Peter died in 1725. He had made many changes in Russia, the church and government as well as the army. Russia also had new money, a new alphabet and calendar. The city of St Petersburg honoured his name, and people called him Peter the Great.

Caught on the reef

With a furious jolt the ship crashed against the reef. Jagged coral splintered the hull and water poured in. Soon the Endeavour was stuck fast. This was surely the end of the ship's voyage. Soon she would be ripped to pieces.

But the captain, James Cook, thought quickly. He sent men below to plug the holes as best they could. Others set about pumping out water. The cannons and heavy equipment were all thrown overboard to make the ship lighter.

Slowly the ship rose until some of the holes made by the reef were showing above the water. And at last, high tide covered the reef and the Endeavour floated clear of the rocks.

They carefully steered the damaged ship to the shore and set to work on the repairs.

Captain Cook and his men had set out from England in 1768 to explore the South Pacific. They had faced storms and even attacks from cannibals but they had survived these and many other great dangers. They had sailed the Endeavour right round New Zealand, the first ship ever to do so. After crossing the Tasman Sea, they landed at Botany Bay in April 1770. Then they had sailed north and now they had come through the largest stretch of coral in the world, the Great Barrier Reef.

After his lucky escape, Cook sailed north again. In August he reached Possession Island off the far north-east of Australia, and claimed the entire east coast of the continent for Great Britain.

Horsemen of the Plains

It was dark as the Indian brave crept slowly forwards. In his hand he gripped a knife. Soon he came to where the horses were tied up, and he cut neatly through the rope that held them. Then, choosing the best horse, he leapt on its back and galloped into the night.

Horses were very important to the Indians who lived on the Plains of North America in the eighteenth and nineteenth centuries. They were the most valuable things they owned. And they were always being stolen – it became a kind of game where sometimes, instead of fighting, tribes would steal each others' horses.

The horses had been brought into the Plains by the Spaniards in the seventeenth century. Once the Indians had horses to ride, they gave up farming and became full-time hunters. They travelled across the huge, flat Plains, hunting the 60 million buffalo that lived there. Horses became the key to success in an Indian tribe, and a person's position depended on the number of horses he owned.

The Plains Indians were magnificent horsemen. Even little boys were taught how to ride without a saddle or stirrups. They could mount running horses just by grasping their manes and jumping up on to their backs.

The age of change

After the Middle Ages, a new age of change began for everyone. In the old days, everything from cloth to nails had been made by hand. Now, machines were being invented—machines that could make these things quickly and cheaply. Thousands of people left their work in the country and flocked to work in factories, minding the new machines. Because the workers had to live close to the factories, houses were built nearby. Shops were opened so that the workers could buy the food and clothes they needed. This is how small towns grew into big cities.

Because the new machines worked so fast, they needed more and more supplies to turn into goods. This is one of the reasons why countries such as Africa were explored, to find new supplies.

The owners of the factories wanted to sell their goods to people

living far away, even overseas. They needed to transport these goods cheaply. So new railways and steamships were built to deliver the goods. The Suez and Panama Canals were dug to make the journeys from country to country much shorter.

The new ships meant that people could travel. Over many years, millions of people left Europe to live elsewhere. Most went to North America.

Another great change happened in the way that people were ruled. The power to rule the country had always been held by a few rich noblemen. Now, in countries such as France and North America, the people took the power away from the rulers. They chose a group of people from amongst themselves to govern the country. They made new rules to make sure that all people were equal, and no single person could rule their country for life. We call this kind of government democracy.

Traders across the sea

During the seventeenth and eighteenth centuries the ports of Europe were humming with activity. The docks were piled high with barrels and cases. Sailors worked busily unloading the ships' holds.

For many years now, ships had been crossing the seas. In earlier times there had been very few, because the journeys were very long and dangerous. But the brave adventurers who came back had brought many new and wonderful luxuries from far-off lands – silk, spices, tobacco, sugar, coffee and tea. The European people wanted more and more of these rich luxuries. So, in time, the owners of the trading ships had got together. They set up great shipping fleets, offices and warehouses for storing goods. The most famous of these organizations were the East India Trading Companies of Britain, France, Holland and Denmark.

The Boston Tea Party

On December 16th 1773 more than a hundred people turned up for a party in Boston, North America. Each one was dressed as an Indian. They went down to the harbour, where they forced their way on board three English ships. Down in the holds, they found the cargo they were looking for – chests and chests of tea. One by one they tipped the contents into the sea.

People jokingly called this the Boston Tea Party. But it wasn't a joke. It was a protest. The Americans were unhappy about being ruled by the British Parliament, because they were not allowed to send any representatives to London to put their point of view. They also thought that the taxes they paid were unfair.

This protest was one of the events that led to the American War of Independence. It took six long years until the British army surrendered. The Americans had won their freedom and the right to make their own laws. And it all started with a tea party!

Sold to be slaves

Another day dawned for the people of the little African village. For them one day was much like any other. The men and women worked in the fields while the children played nearby.

But this day did not turn out to be like other days. Suddenly, as the people prepared to go to the fields, a large number of men stormed into the village. Using guns and whips they drove the men, women and children together. Those who tried to fight back were beaten or killed.

In a short time the invaders had all their prisoners tied together in a long line. Then they set out for the distant coast. On the long march many of the prisoners died. Their bodies were left where they fell.

When they reached the coast, the villagers stared in wonder at the great ocean before them. Never had they seen anything like it. But before they had time to do much more than look, they were herded aboard a great ship. The slave traders – for this is what the invaders were – pushed everyone down a hatch into the dark hold of the ship. There even the women with babies were put in chains so that they could barely move.

The next day the ship set sail for America, thousands of kilometres away. Once each day the captives were taken up on deck for exercise and a little food and water. The rest of the time they lay in chains in the dark hold. Many who became ill on the voyage were thrown overboard.

These poor Africans were to be sold into slavery. In America they would be put to work on sugar and cotton plantations. Never again would they know the freedom they had in their village.

During some 300 years, many millions of Africans were sold as slaves in North and South America and the West Indies. In 1807 the British were the first to outlaw the slave trade, but this did not stop slavery. It took another eighty years before slavery came to an end in the western world.

March to the palace

"We want bread! We want bread!"

It was October 1789. The people of Paris were on the march and this was their chant. They were poor and hungry. Every day they had to queue at the bakers' shops to buy bread, but there was never enough. The wheat harvest had failed and there was not enough bread to go round.

So the hungry people had decided to take action. They were marching to the palace of their king, Louis XVI of France. They carried guns, axes and spears with them. No one was going to stop them!

When they reached the palace of Versailles, the king came out to see them. He promised that they should have more bread to eat, but promises weren't enough for the angry crowd. That night they broke into the palace, and the king was forced to run away with his wife and son. But the next day the royal family was captured and taken back to Paris. The king was the prisoner of the people. Now, surely, they would have plenty to eat.

But things were not that simple. The people of France didn't just want more food, they wanted to change the way their country was controlled. The rich nobles had land and money, but they paid hardly any taxes, while the poor had to pay taxes for many things — even salt! If the king would not help the poor, they would get rid of him. And that is exactly what happened. Three years later, the king was put to death and the French people had power in their own hands at last.

Victory for Napoleon

"A new general is coming! He will lead us to victory!" The French troops hoped that the news was right.

The year was 1796, and these soldiers were camped at the foot of the Alps, just outside northern Italy. They had been sent there several years before to drive the Austrian army out of the regions called Lombardy and Piedmont. But so far they had failed. Their clothes were in rags, and they had barely enough food . What could a new general do?

In fact, he led them to victory. The general was Napoleon Bonaparte. He was only twenty-six years old and little more than one and a half metres tall, but he inspired the tired soldiers. Using clever new battle plans, he managed to push the Austrians further and further east. And, at last, his victorious army marched into Milan, the capital of Lombardy.

Napoleon's victory made him very popular with the French army. Soon that popularity spread among the ordinary French people, and when the government became unpopular, and were thrown out, Napoleon was declared First Consul of all France.

Napoleon's success in battles and in government continued for many years. He finally conquered an empire even larger than that of Charlemagne and Caesar.

But in the end, Napoleon tried to extend the borders of his empire too far. He failed to conquer England and Spain, and suffered a terrible defeat in Russia. The European countries joined together to defeat Napoleon.

This grand arch was built in Milan in 1807.
It honours Napoleon's victory over the Austrian army.

Colony of thieves

Simeon Lord was a thief. He'd stolen two
bundles of cloth, and for this he was sent to
prison. But in England, where he lived, all the
jails were full. So Simeon was sent to the other
side of the world – to Australia!

He was locked in a transport ship, crowded
with more than a hundred other convicts.
In 1791 the ship landed at Sydney Cove, in
Australia. As Simeon walked down the
gang-plank, he stared about him at the strange
new land. The sun beat down fiercely on to the
shore, where a few rough huts stood. Behind
them were dusty fields and huge forests.
Simeon blinked in the strong light. This was to
be his home for seven long years.

Simeon Lord was one of the earliest of the
British convicts to be transported to Australia.
The first shipload had arrived in 1788. At that
time there were only a few white settlers in the
country. Most of the people living there were
Aborigines, who'd been in Australia for
hundreds of years.

During the next eighty years, thousands of
criminals were sent out from Britain. Life for
them was very hard. They were sent to work in
the fields or on building sites. Many died,
either because they were worn out through
hard work and eating so little, or because of
disease. But a few managed to survive and do
well.

Simeon Lord was one of the lucky ones.
After his seven years as a prisoner he was set
free, but he didn't go back to England. Instead,

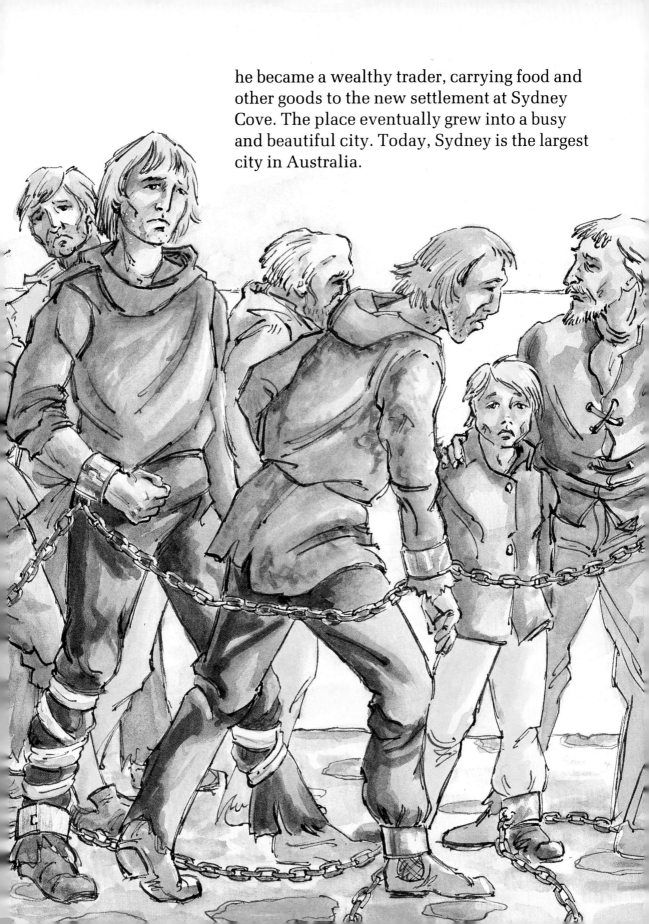

he became a wealthy trader, carrying food and other goods to the new settlement at Sydney Cove. The place eventually grew into a busy and beautiful city. Today, Sydney is the largest city in Australia.

The coming of the railways

Snorting and roaring, the metal monster came thundering by. Smoke poured from its funnel and steam hissed from its pistons. The earth shook. Everyone rushed to catch a glimpse of the great machine as it passed. Workers in the nearby fields threw down their tools, women hurried out of their houses and children ran from play to look.

The year was 1830. Very few people in Britain had ever seen a steam engine before, but now a passenger line had been built between Liverpool and Manchester. When a train passed by, crowds came to watch. Many of them were terrified – the engine made such a noise, and it travelled so fast!

Some people were afraid that the railways would bring disaster to the countryside. They thought the crops would be ruined by smoke and sparks, or that the cows would die of shock. Others believed the trains would spoil the landscape with their noise and ugliness.

But railways had come to stay. In a few years there were hundreds of new lines being built all over Britain. People soon became used to the sights and sounds of the steam train. And, for the first time in history, people were able to travel long distances very quickly.

Children at work

Are you scared of the dark? Just think how dark it must be at the bottom of a coal mine. The only light is the glow of a candle which might be blown out by a draught of air at any time.

You stand in the darkness from early morning to late at night. You're getting numb, but you can't move away because you have a job to do. Whenever you hear a wagonload of coal coming down the tunnel towards you, you must open a door to let it pass and close the door again once it is through. During the day you will eat a slice of bread spread with fat and listen to the rats scratching round for crumbs.

Thousands of little girls and boys lived like this in Britain during the eighteenth and early nineteenth centuries. There were few schools, and working people were so poor that their children often had to go to work to help out. Much of the work that children did was hard and dangerous. Children working in the mines might be crushed by the coal wagons, and the stale air and lack of sunshine made them weak and ill.

It was not until 1842 that a law was passed to stop mine owners from employing children underground. But in factories and mills there were still other jobs for children to do, and they were just as tiring and dangerous.

Gold fever

It's hard to keep a secret – especially when you don't want people to know you've just found a fortune in gold! When John Sutter found gold on his land in California he tried hard to keep quiet, but within a year the news had leaked out.

Almost immediately, the rush began. During 1849 thousands of people from all over the world made their way to California. They left their farms, their shops and factories, and rushed to California to make their fortune. Some came by ship, others trekked across plains and mountains. Every one of them had gold fever.

Many of these 'forty-niners', as they were called, lost their lives on the terrible journey to California. Some died of starvation or disease, and some were killed by Indians. Those who did get there found life very hard. The first to arrive grabbed the richest pieces of land, but in the end, very few gold-seekers made their fortunes.

Gold-seekers used pans to scoop up mud from the river beds. Sometimes they found grains of gold amongst the pebbles.

The lady with the lamp

Florence Nightingale was rich and beautiful. Nearly every evening she was invited out to dinner or to a dance. London in the 1850s was a good place to live if you had plenty of money.

But was Florence happy? Not really. Deep inside she wanted to do something useful and help others. She decided that she was going to work in a hospital. Her mother was horrified, because at that time hospitals were dirty, smelly places. They had no proper bathrooms or lavatories and the nurses were rough and untrained. A hospital was no place for a gentle young woman to work.

But Florence had made up her mind. She went to work at a nursing home in London. And then in 1854, she found a greater challenge. The British army was fighting a war in the Crimea, on the Black Sea. The sick and wounded soldiers were sent to an army hospital in nearby Turkey. With a band of nurses, Florence sailed out to look after them.

The women were shocked by what they found. The hospital was a terrible place – far worse than hospitals in England. The patients were packed together and many lay on blankets on the mud. There were no fires and hardly any water or food. The doctors didn't have enough medicines or bandages. Out of every thousand patients, 420 died.

At first the army doctors weren't quite sure of Florence because they'd never had nurses in their hospitals before. But Florence set to work. She had the floors scrubbed and the drains cleaned. She arranged for food, clothes and medicines to be sent out.

Every night she walked through the wards carrying a little lamp. She would stop and speak to any soldier who couldn't sleep or who was in pain. They called her the lady with the lamp.

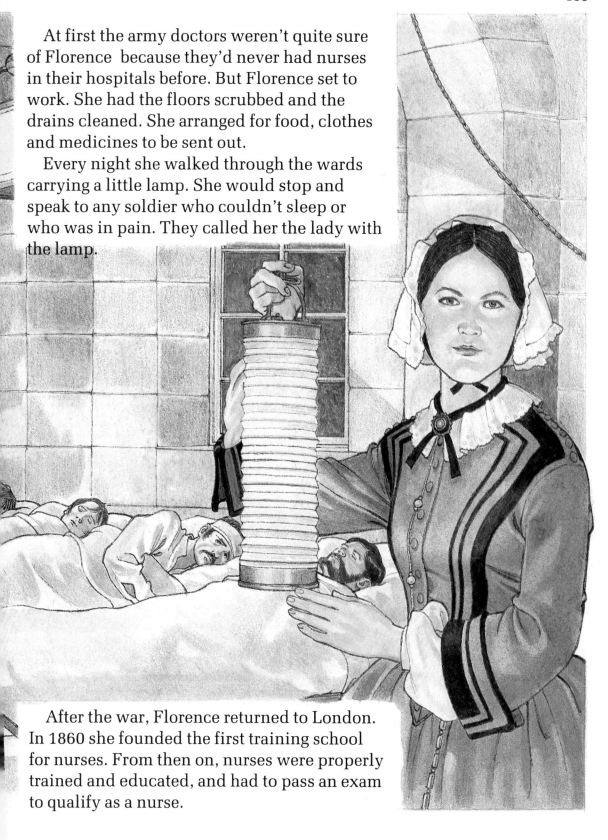

After the war, Florence returned to London. In 1860 she founded the first training school for nurses. From then on, nurses were properly trained and educated, and had to pass an exam to qualify as a nurse.

Meeting at Ujiji

"Find Livingstone!"

It sounded straightforward enough. The year was 1869, and Henry Stanley, who worked for a New York newspaper, had been told to go to Africa. His task was to look for a man called David Livingstone. He could have as much money and equipment as he needed for the journey – but he must succeed.

But finding Livingstone was not easy. Dr David Livingstone was a very famous man in Britain, although he hadn't lived there for many years. He was working in Central Africa as a doctor and missionary, helping sick people and teaching Christianity. He had also explored huge areas of Africa where no European had ever been before. But now he seemed to have vanished and many people believed he was dead.

Henry Stanley prepared carefully for his trip. He took with him six tonnes of supplies – including an enamel bath and a Persian carpet! All this needed over 200 men to carry it.

The journey was terrible. At one time, the party had to wade through a swamp where mud came up to their necks. Another time, Stanley was attacked by a crocodile. He became weak with fever, but still he trudged on.

At last Stanley reached Ujiji, the village from which news of Livingstone had last been heard. In the middle of the village stood the man they'd been looking for. Henry Stanley stepped forward, lifted his hat and spoke the famous words:

"Dr Livingstone, I presume?"

Short-cut through Suez

Boom! A massive explosion split the air. Rocks and mud shot into the sky and the dam broke. Ferdinand de Lesseps watched the swirling waters proudly. At last the Suez Canal was complete.

It was August 16th 1869. De Lesseps, a French engineer, had been given the job of building the new waterway fifteen years before. It had been very hard work for all the thousands of builders who had carried out his plans. In some places they had to blast through solid rock. In others they had to scoop up mud, squeeze the water from it and build it into the walls. And all the while the heat was terrific.

Now the canal was finished. It stretched for 165 kilometres and formed a link between the Mediterranean Sea in the north and the Red Sea in the south. Soon the first cargo ships were sailing through.

Why was the Suez Canal so important? The answer is that it made a short-cut between Europe and Asia. Instead of sailing all the way round Africa, ships could slip through the canal straight into the Indian Ocean. The journey to India no longer took three months but only three weeks.

Take-off at Kitty Hawk

Wilbur and Orville Wright of Dayton, Ohio, in the USA owned a small bicycle factory and loved to tinker with machines and build things.

In 1899, they began building gliders. They used some new ideas to make a machine that would fly under its own power, instead of depending on the wind to make it move. To do this they had to build their own very small, light engine, which they hooked up to two propellors. Their flying machine was a rickety thing with two pairs of large wings made of cloth and bits of wood tied together with wire.

Wilbur and Orville took this machine, called Flyer, to Kitty Hawk in North Carolina, where they flew all their gliders. This was a broad, flat, sandy place with no trees, where a strong wind was almost always blowing.

On the morning of December 17th 1903, Flyer's little engine was started and Orville crawled on to the wing. "All set," he called to Wilbur.

"Let her go," shouted Wilbur.

Orville unfastened the wire that held the machine. Its propellors whirring, Flyer began to roll slowly along the track. Then the machine picked up speed and surged forward. Two-thirds of the way along the track, it lifted into the air.

Peering down, Orville saw the ground slipping swiftly past, three metres beneath him. He was flying – the first man to fly in an engine-powered, heavier-than-air flying machine, the kind we now call an aeroplane.

The last wilderness

Antarctica is a wild and beautiful place. The whole land is covered with ice and snow, except where high mountains push through the frozen surface. Bitter winds blow and hardly anything grows. In winter, temperatures drop as low as -60°C.

Ernest Shackleton, an Irishman, was determined to be the first to cross the bleak land. In 1914 he set out in a ship called the Endurance. But that winter the ship was frozen into the icy sea many kilometres from the shore. Slowly the ship was crushed and began to sink. So Shackleton and his men were forced to camp out on the ice.

There now began one of the most amazing sea journeys ever made. Shackleton's party

was a long way from any help. All that the men had were three small boats and some food. So they pulled the boats to the open sea and made their way to the nearest island. No one lived there, of course, and there was nothing to eat except penguins.

Shackleton knew he'd have to do something else if they were to survive. He chose five men and sailed off in the strongest boat. It was tiny, but it travelled 1,300 kilometres across the stormiest seas in the world. Somehow, after terrible dangers, the crew reached the island of South Georgia. Shackleton crossed the island, over mountains and glaciers, and managed to find help.

Shackleton saved his men, but he failed to cross Antarctica. Many other explorers failed too, and it was not until 1958 that an expedition led by Sir Vivian Fuchs managed to cross the icy wastes. The last wilderness had finally been conquered.

Christmas stops the war

It was Christmas morning in 1914. The sky was blue over the French countryside and there was no wind. On the battlefield, all was quiet. No guns fired, no bombs burst.

Carefully the soldier pulled himself up to look over the top of the trench. "Had the war finished?" he wondered. Usually he wouldn't have dared to show his head – the enemy would have shot at him. But today was different.

As he watched he saw something even more surprising. Some of the enemy soldiers were climbing out of their trenches. They had no guns with them and they were strolling towards him. He looked back at his own lines and saw some of his comrades going out to meet the enemy.

The two groups met half-way. On one side were the Germans, and on the other were the

British. They shook hands and chatted as well as they could in their different languages. Only yesterday they had been trying to kill each other, and today they were friends!

Later that day the two sides played a football match. They showed each other photographs of their families and gave Christmas presents. But the peace was not allowed to last long. The senior officers on each side were angry that the war had stopped, and next day the guns began firing again.

This war, now called the First World War, lasted for four more years. Millions of men on both sides were killed, and many others were badly wounded. But those who had taken part in the Christmas peace of 1914 never forgot the day when they'd made friends with their enemies.

Return of a revolutionary

As the train stopped, a carriage door opened and out stepped a short man. A great shout went up from thousands of people who'd gathered there to greet him. It was April 16th 1917, and Lenin had come back to Russia.

Lenin was given a hero's welcome because he was the leader of a group of people called the Bolsheviks. This was one of several groups who had been trying to get rid of the Russian tsar or king, and rule the country themselves. The tsar had wanted to put Lenin in prison, but Lenin had escaped to Switzerland. Since then, the people had risen up against the tsar, and in March he had given up his throne. A government was put in his place. But this wasn't enough for the Bolsheviks. They wanted to take the land away from the rich people. It would be owned by the government, but not by this new government, which was ruled by a prince.

So Lenin had come back. He had to fight hard to organize the revolution. His powerful speeches soon persuaded the people. They were starving, they had no land to farm, and millions of men had been killed in the First World War, which was still going on. The Bolshevik slogan was simple – "Peace, land and bread". The three things that the people wanted.

After many struggles, the Bolsheviks took the city of Moscow in November 1917. Lenin had led them to victory.

The great salt march

"Where are you all going?"

"To the coast."

"But that's over 200 kilometres away! Why are you going there?"

"To make salt."

The long line of marchers moved on across India. Most of them carried pots and pans. At their head walked Mohandas Gandhi, the man they called Mahatma, or Great Soul. He wore only a loin cloth, and carried a staff in his hand.

The marchers reached Dandi, on the west coast, in April 1930. They filled their pans with sea water. Then, as it got dark, they lit great fires on the seashore and boiled the water on these until only the salt was left.

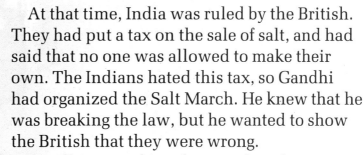

At that time, India was ruled by the British. They had put a tax on the sale of salt, and had said that no one was allowed to make their own. The Indians hated this tax, so Gandhi had organized the Salt March. He knew that he was breaking the law, but he wanted to show the British that they were wrong.

Gandhi wanted much more than that. He wanted the British to go home and leave the Indians to govern themselves. But he didn't start a war about it. Because he was a man of peace, he made his protests peacefully. It was many years before British rule ended, and Gandhi was put in prison many times for his views. But at last his dream came true. In 1947 India became an independent nation.

During the bombing raids of the Second World War, many European families hid in home-made **shelters**.

Searchlights pin-pointed enemy bombers so that anti-aircraft gunners could see their targets. If the shells missed a plane, they exploded in the air.

Air raid!

It was midnight and all over the city the sirens began to wail. This warning noise meant there was going to be an air raid!

The little girl was woken by the siren. She ran downstairs with her parents and out into the garden. There, half-buried in the earth, was the shelter. They hurried in and shut the door, and soon they heard the drone of the aeroplanes overhead. Then – crump! – the ground shook as the bombs began to fall.

The little girl was soon tucked into her own bed in the shelter. Next to her there was a little night-light, in case she was afraid. She didn't like being in the shelter, even though it was a safe place. It was hot and stuffy inside. Water leaked in through the sides, and black beetles crawled across the ceiling and fell on top of her. Sometimes she had to stay there for hours.

During the Second World War, which began in 1939, there were thousands of air raids. Towns all over Europe were damaged by bombs, and thousands of men, women and children were killed. This was the first time that war had put everyone in danger. In the past, it was only the soldiers on the battlefield who were likely to be killed.

Many families built shelters in their gardens. Those who didn't, ran to public shelters. Some even spent the night in underground railway stations – anywhere to be safe from the bombs.

Today's events, tomorrow's history

In this book we have come through thousands of years of history. And now we have reached today. So this page is really about you, because you are reading it today.

You are a part of history, because history never stops. It goes on being made, year after year. What is happening today will be history in a few years' time.

Imagine you could leap forward one thousand years. The people alive then will wonder what life was like in your lifetime. Children in school may be taught about the primitive spacecraft that reached the moon, the old-fashioned way of using petrol fuel to power cars, or even a weird musical sound made with guitars and drums which young people hopped up and down to.

Perhaps you could be of help to the archaeologists of tomorrow's world. Take a large waterproof, plastic container and label it **'Time Capsule of the year ' collected by young historian ....** Fill in the date and your name.

In the container place cuttings and objects which you believe will give future historians a clue to the events of your lifetime – a photo of the way you dress, a bus or train ticket, postcards of your area as it is today, labels of popular foods and drinks, newspaper cuttings about famous people and events, a list of popular TV programmes, and so on.

Place your Time Capsule somewhere safe where it may be found in a thousand years' time.

Index

This index is an alphabetical list of the important words and topics in this book.

When you are looking for a special piece of information, you can look for the word in the list and it will tell you which pages to look at.

If you do not find what you want in this index, you can look at the General Index in Volume 16. This gives a list for all the books in **Childcraft**.

Acknowledgement

The publishers of **Childcraft** gratefully acknowledge the following artists, photographers, publishers, agencies and corporations for illustrations used in this volume. All illustrations are the exclusive property of the publishers of **Childcraft** unless names are marked with an asterisk *.

Cover	Charles Front

6–7	Terry Thomas (Specs Art Agency)	76–77	Charles Front
8–9	Charles Front	78–79	Susan Hunter (Young Artists)
10–11	Richard Hook	80–83	Charles Front
14–15	Jacqueline Rogers	84–85	Roy King (Specs Art Agency)
16–17	Susan Hunter (Young Artists)	86–87	Terry Thomas (Specs Art Agency)
18–19	Terry Thomas (Specs Art Agency)	88–89	Nigel Alexander (Specs Art Agency)
20–21	Charles Front		
22–23	Sowyer's Inc; Robert Harding Picture Library*	90–93	Roy King (Specs Art Agency)
		94–95	Charles Front
24–25	Roy King (Specs Art Agency)	96–97	Duncan Harper
26–27	Duncan Harper	98–99	Gerald Witcomb (Specs Art Agency)
28–29	Zefa Picture Library*		
30–31	Roy King (Specs Art Agency)	100–101	Charles Front
32–33	Richard Hook	102–103	Michael Strand (B.L. Kearley Ltd)
34–35	Jeremy Gower (B.L. Kearley Ltd); Richard Hook	104–105	Roy King (Specs Art Agency)
		106–109	Susan Hunter (Young Artists)
36–37	Charles Front; Fiona Pragoff*	110–111	Gerald Witcomb (Specs Art Agency)
38–39	Norman Tomalin (Bruce Coleman Ltd*)		
		112–113	Roy King (Specs Art Agency)
40–41	Terry Thomas (Specs Art Agency)	114–115	Terry Thomas (Specs Art Agency)
42–43	Roy King (Specs Art Agency)	116–117	Max Ranft
44–45	Susan Hunter (Young Artists)	118–119	Donald Harley (B.L. Kearley Ltd)
46–49	Charles Front	120–121	Roy King (Specs Art Agency)
50–51	Roy King (Specs Art Agency)	122–123	Charles Front
52–53	Ted Fairburn (Specs Art Agency)	124–125	Overseas - Agenzia fotografica s.r.l.
54–55	Nigel Alexander (Specs Art Agency)		
		126–127	Roy King (Specs Art Agency)
56–57	Susan Hunter (Young Artists)	128–131	Duncan Harper
58–59	Brian Nash (Zefa Picture Library*)	132–133	Roy King (Specs Art Agency)
60–61	Susan Hunter (Young Artists)	134–135	Pat Tourret (B.L. Kearley Ltd)
62–63	Terry Thomas (Specs Art Agency)	136–137	Charles Front
64–65	Charles Front	138–139	Duncan Harper
66–67	Max Ranft	140–141	Richard Hook
68–69	Roy King (Specs Art Agency)	142–143	Ted Fairburn (Specs Art Agency)
70–71	Photri (Robert Harding Picture Library*)	144–145	Susan Hunter (Young Artists)
		146–147	Tony Herbert (B.L. Kearley Ltd)
72–73	Charles Front	148–149	Terry Thomas (Specs Art Agency)
74–75	Nigel Alexander (Specs Art Agency)	150–151	Duncan Harper
		152–153	Gary Slater (Specs Art Agency)